THE PAINTED FURNITURE

SOURCEBOOK

ANNIE SLOAN

THE PAINTED FURNITURE
SOURCEBOOK

MOTIFS FROM MEDIEVAL TIMES TO THE PRESENT DAY

RIZZOLI
NEW YORK

First published in the United States of America in 1998
by Rizzoli International Publications, Inc.
300 Park Avenue South, New York 10010

First published in Great Britain in 1998
by Collins & Brown Limited

ISBN 0-8478-2120-X

LC 98-65886

Editor: Alison Wormleighton
Designer: Christine Wood

Reproduction by Grafiscan, Italy
Printed in Hong Kong by Midas Printing Ltd

(*Frontispiece*) In Switzerland, as in many Northern European countries where timber was plentiful and used extensively in rooms, the wood was painted. This room in the Château de Rougemont, Switzerland, has been painted to relieve the monotony of what would otherwise be unrelenting brown wood. Simple landscapes and scenes from heroic and religious tales adorn the panels, surrounded by painted scroll "carving". The mouldings and columns have been painted with a very impressionistic marble.

Contents

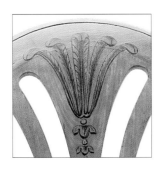
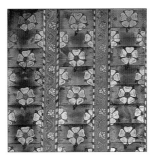

Introduction

THE PHOTOGRAPHS IN THIS BOOK are a personal mix of painted furniture and walls that I have come across in one way or another over the years. Some of the places I have visited and others I have read about, while still others I have heard about on the grapevine. It is not meant to be a complete history, or the book would be enormous. I know there will be some terrific rooms and some delectable pieces of furniture that I have missed, whether through ignorance or difficulty in getting photographs. This book is simply a collection of painted works that I like.

In it I have tried to a show a wide variety of styles and to cover a little of the history of the subject. There are five sections, representing the broad areas into which decoration can be divided. It has been interesting to see how sometimes a motif, particularly the bell flower, will pop up again and again in all sorts of interpretations – neat and clear and tight, as at Osterley Park in London; loose and extravagant, as at the Swedish artist Carl Larsson's home; elegant on chinoiserie cabinets; or naïve on Alpine chests.

Rich traditions

With the exception of some stunning photographs from India and one from Mexico, the painted furniture and walls all come from either Europe or America. Every country has its tradition of painted work but some countries' traditions are more highly developed than others. Scandinavia, particularly Sweden, has a rich history of painted interiors and furniture, centring mainly on an intense period of activity in the eighteenth century. Their tradition is highly individual and immediately recognizable. The work is often strongly coloured, using a particular range of blues and orange-pinks in designs that tend to be very confident and large-scale. These decorative ideas spread as the decorators travelled and as a result of trading links.

Other parts of Europe – often areas where wood was plentiful, like Germany, Hungary, Poland, Switzerland and Austria – also had lively traditions of painted work. In some regions, such as the country areas of Holland, the patterns of the past are still practised. In England and France the country tradition was less strong but it is from here that some of the finest works in the classical tradition emerged. Delicate craftsmanship with chinoiserie lacquerwork, gilding, hand-painting and

faux finishes on walls and furniture were all carried out in grand country houses and châteaux. Influential designers such as Thomas Chippendale and Robert Adam used a great deal of painted decoration.

Italy has the longest tradition of painted works, and the oldest piece of painted furniture included in this book is a *cassone*, a type of marriage chest, which dates from about the fourteenth century. Many different styles of painting are found in Italy, from simple country chests to palaces with *trompe l'oeil* decoration. Because Venice was an important trading port with the east, Italy was able to absorb a great diversity of ideas. This, combined with already highly developed craftsmanship, led to imaginative ideas such as *lacca povera* – exquisite decoration using paper cut-outs – as well as works with intricate classical motifs and gilding.

On the other side of the Atlantic, settlers who had come from all over Northern Europe were bringing traditions, pattern books and in some cases even the actual wooden cupboards and chests. Most of the early painted American work was decorated by settlers from Germany, hence the term Pennsylvania German (or Pennsylvania Dutch, a corruption of the word *deutsch*) to describe this particular work. As the years went by the work gradually changed, incorporating new motifs and materials, to become distinctively American.

The hand of the artist

My own style tends to be loose and direct, with as little planning as I can possibly get away with. For this reason I love the work of the Bloomsbury Group, especially Duncan Grant and Vanessa Bell, who lived and worked at Charleston in East Sussex, England, and employed a loose style of brushwork. With any work where the brush marks are freely applied, you can almost feel the hand of the person who did them all those years ago, bringing the artist and their work close to you.

You will find lots of folk- or country-painted pieces of furniture here. I tend to like what may be called the more crudely painted pieces, as sometimes folk painting can be too formula-led and as a result dead-looking. Some of the painted chests in particular are so personal and idiosyncratic that you almost feel like you know the owners.

In Friesland, in the northern Netherlands, the traditional folk painting is known as Hindeloopen. The usual colours for the base are a dark green, a rich deep blue or the deep claret on this folded table (*above*).

The walls and ceilings of this merchant's house (*pages 6-7*) in Scotland, were painted in about 1620, using earth pigments.

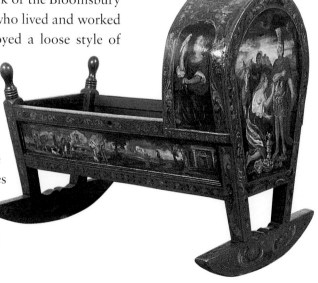

This is one of many rooms painted at Culross Palace, in Scotland (*above*). Here the barrel-ceilinged room has been painted with sixteen allegorical panels, each with a moral text.

The child that rested in this painted cradle (*opposite below*) from the Netherlands was obviously intended for great things. In the panels there are finely painted scenes from classical and heroic tales and around the panels are classical motifs painted in a folk style.

Sources of inspiration

My other criteria for inclusion in the book was whether an item could be used to inspire painted decorations in today's house. For this reason I haven't included either very grand work or church interiors, and I have tried to have a mix of decoration executed by amateurs and professional artists. The work that has been carefully planned skilfully and organized and expertly carried out, such as the painting on the walls at Attingham Park, is something to aspire to.

I hope looking at this book will inspire you to paint and to use the designs as a springboard for your own designs. We have tried as much as possible throughout the book to show designs clearly so that you can copy, trace or photostat them. At the back of the book I have included lots of motifs, some taken from the furniture in the book and some from an amalgam of other pieces. Artists and decorators have always built upon other people's motifs and decorative ideas. Copy the motifs directly, change them a little or enlarge them – you will soon make the painting your own.

Fruits and flowers

Flowers in bloom or bud, fruits in bowls or bunches, and leaves on twigs or trees are used in profusion on furniture and walls. They are the mainstays of painted decoration, both classical and informal, painted loosely or in a stylized way. Some motifs crop up again and again, such as the vase of flowers, seen in classical gilded splendour on an eighteenth-century chinoiserie cabinet, on the panel of a Swiss country cupboard and in a niche in an Indian wall.

Particular flowers such as roses and tulips have always been popular with folk painters and can be represented with just a few deft brush strokes.

Flowers, fruits and leaves offer a variety of colour and shape and are flexible. A posy or a length of vine can be adapted to any shape by adding another leaf or flower here and there.

The very strong motifs in this room use only a few colours. Set against a bleached wooden floor and off-white walls, the main colours are olive green and grey-blue which are cool and restful on the eye. The warm, slightly muted pinkish orange brings everything together, adding little bursts of warmth. The designs have been hand-painted but this could be done using stencils with hand-painting to give the motifs a non-repetitive look.

The dado has been spattered but could be sponged in shades of grey-blue. The patina could be achieved using either a brownish wash, coloured varnishes or waxes of different intensities.

Some of the finest painted interiors in the world can be found in Sweden. Most of these were painted in the eighteenth century and can be found in places ranging from simple country farmhouses to grand palaces. Painters worked by travelling around the country and offering painted interiors in exchange for board and lodging and a small payment. There would often be a room in a house where important events, such as weddings, christenings or special birthdays or anniversaries would be celebrated. The room would be painted by the itinerant decorator according to various themes.

The main focus of this Swedish room is the blue crown motifs. These sit on stripy pedestals and act like vases from which flowers and leaves spring. Linking the whole room, a cream monochrome swag is intertwined with a leafy garland and hung from tall columns. The decorator probably owned many stencils which were put together in different ways according to the job. The leaves may have been stencilled in green first and then outlined in black, resulting in slight variations in the design.

FRUITS AND FLOWERS

Grapes and vine leaves (*below*) were particular favourites for chair backs, with the spiral-shaped tendrils acting as a decorative device. The designs usually have a central focus, are more or less symmetrical and aim for a decorative rather than a realistic look. The decoration is generally contained and framed in a painted panel. Few colours were used for the decoration, and warm cream or yellow was common for the background. Painted lines emphasized the contours of the piece. For hand-painted lines use a fine long-haired brush that will hold a lot of paint. Or make thin lines using two rows of masking tape set very close together, then apply very dry paint. Remove the tape immediately.

The back of a chair provides the perfect place for decorative effects depicting anything from flowers or fruit to landscapes or classical motifs. Early American settlers, many from northern Europe where folk-painted furniture was common, soon developed their own style. These two American chairs, both dating from about 1830, were stencilled and hand-painted, the one on the right by John D. Pratt of Lunenburg, Massachusetts.

This dressing table (*opposite*), painted in 1835 by Grover Spooner, uses a bright yellow ochre as the base, with stencil designs done mainly in solid terracotta. On the shaped back the stencilled bowl of fruit has a little white added and the paint has been applied less solidly. Part of the charm of this table is the uneven quality of the painted designs. For a similar effect, try stamping the design using a cut sponge or even a cut potato, then rub back when the paint is dry.

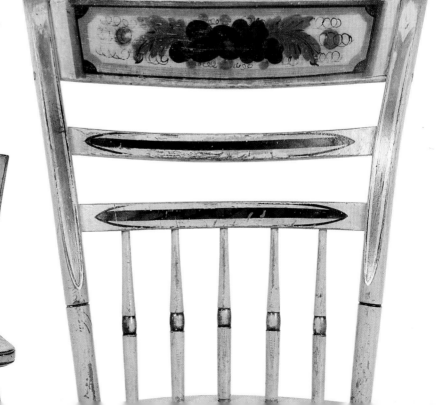

Charleston in East Sussex, England, was the home of artists Vanessa Bell and Duncan Grant from 1916. Most of the surfaces were decorated. On a cupboard door in a bathroom (*opposite*) a lively, bold vase of flowers was painted by their daughter Angelica Garnett in the 1930s, using loose and expressive brushwork. There are many ideas here that could be taken up by non-artists. Circles, dots, squares, lines and the loose abstracted version of a garland could be done freehand or with printing materials. Print using cork ends, jar lids, the edges of pieces of very thick cardboard, or cut sponges to get the spontaneous, slightly uneven look of this style. The chair next to the cupboard, by contrast, uses a lot of colours with more controlled brushwork. It was painted in 1974 by Richard Shone, a protégé of Duncan Grant.

FRUITS AND FLOWERS

In a shallow niche of a wall in Rajasthan, India, is a simple, still and calm painting of a vase of flowers (*left*). Set against a clear, airy pink, the vase, with its strong colours and its slight shading, is pleasingly solid by contrast. The perfectly symmetrical all-white flowers and leaves look as though they might float away.

The very basic vases of flowers bursting out from under the arches on this American dower chest painted in 1785 in Berks County, Pennsylvania (*below*), are charmingly naïve. The tulips are portly, the pillars are top-heavy and rows of fat red hearts are folded around the corners, with spindly tulips poking their heads out from between each one. Deep green with pinkish terracotta is a lively mixture made possible by using a very pale cream as an outline. The design could have been done using stencils to pencil in the position of the symmetrical design, then filling in with colour by hand, which would account for the slight differences in shape. Use an off-white or beige to outline the design. Finally rub back the paintwork.

This Italian eighteenth-century hand-painted bureau is decorated on every possible surface. On the drawers (*left*) the same motifs are used in different ways, adding to the simple liveliness. Simple pink carnations and leaves form a playful arch around the keyholes, but it is the blue and yellow rococo scrolls that give it such a stylish look. Near the handles on the first and third drawers, note the blue lattice-work, a device that makes an area solid without looking heavy. On the doors the design is softer and more whimsical, as if the foliage is twisting around the edge (*right*). The base is likely to have been white originally, over a gesso ground, with red and deep green plants, and blues and ochres for the decoration. It would have been finished with varnish, which has yellowed over the years. Nowadays water-based paints can be used, finishing with a coloured patination using wax or varnish.

This stunning red japanned bureau-bookcase must have seemed shockingly bright and exotic in 1720 when it arrived at Erddig House, Clwyd, Wales. The vermilion red, which has faded on the outside to a dull, warm orange, would have been deep, glossy and intense, as it still is on the inside of the cabinet. This piece was made in England but the shiny gold brushwork decorations are intricate Eastern motifs. The design on the inner door panel (*left*) shows an elegant but decidedly Oriental arrangement of flowers, with jagged stems and long blades of grass projecting out to give balance. The willow in the small

panel of the desk (*below right*) is very sparsely described, showing only three branches in a manner which is realistic and yet stylized. The decoration on the drawer front (*below*) uses three separate motifs which are not in scale with each other but which nevertheless work because of the balance of size and colour.

Original Oriental lacquerwork was achieved using a time-consuming and painstaking method of applying numerous alternating coloured and uncoloured coats of a shellac-type varnish, rubbed down between each layer. The secret of achieving a fine lacquered look involved much debate in Europe in the seventeenth and eighteenth centuries. Japanning, named in homage to the East, was the European interpretation. Black was the original colour for lacquerwork but red, yellow, white, deep blue and olive green were also used for both lacquerwork and japanning.

This American painted chair (*right*), done about 1820 in Salem, Massachusetts, is in imitation of chinoiserie pieces but has been painted very simply. A shiny red paint has been used as the base, and the Chinese-inspired designs have been produced using stencils and bronze powder instead of raised gold.

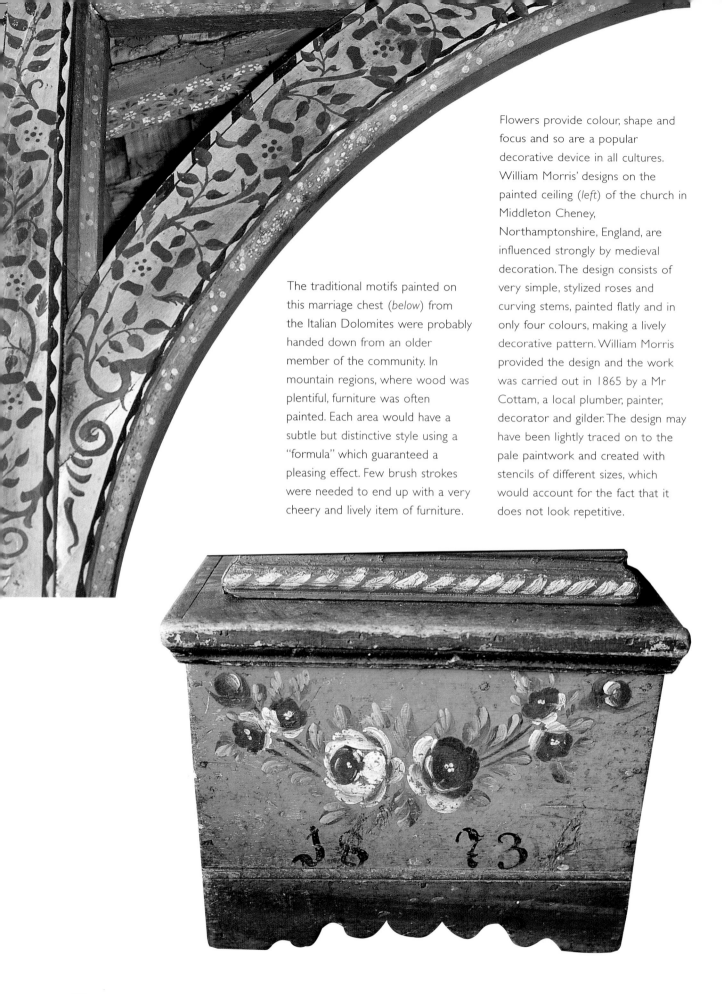

The traditional motifs painted on this marriage chest (*below*) from the Italian Dolomites were probably handed down from an older member of the community. In mountain regions, where wood was plentiful, furniture was often painted. Each area would have a subtle but distinctive style using a "formula" which guaranteed a pleasing effect. Few brush strokes were needed to end up with a very cheery and lively item of furniture.

Flowers provide colour, shape and focus and so are a popular decorative device in all cultures. William Morris' designs on the painted ceiling (*left*) of the church in Middleton Cheney, Northamptonshire, England, are influenced strongly by medieval decoration. The design consists of very simple, stylized roses and curving stems, painted flatly and in only four colours, making a lively decorative pattern. William Morris provided the design and the work was carried out in 1865 by a Mr Cottam, a local plumber, painter, decorator and gilder. The design may have been lightly traced on to the pale paintwork and created with stencils of different sizes, which would account for the fact that it does not look repetitive.

FRUITS AND FLOWERS

In this dressing room (*left*) at Sweden's Drottningholm Court Theatre, near Stockholm, the hand-painted wallpaper in the Chinese style dates from the eighteenth century. The trees are simplified and the flowers are simply clusters of white petals outlined and hatched with a pale olive green to suggest shading. The design is stylized but the overall effect is realistic. To help focus our eyes on the decoration, discreet pale blue birds, in the same tone as the leaves, and marked in the same way, are perched on branches. The leaf motif with the spiralling tendril (*see detail, above*) is similar to designs found in Swedish folk-painted furniture and on American pieces.

23

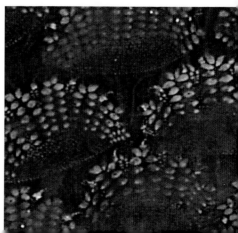

This stylized plant form (*right*) found at the Sigtia Haveli in Rajasthan, India, could be either flowers in a vase or a tree. In India there are many forms of these tree of life plants, often found near doorways like decorations. Usually the painter will have memorized the design and so will have painted it freehand without stencils.

The walls and ceilings of corridors, halls and resting rooms in the Samode Palace (*left*), Rajasthan, India, were stunningly painted and decorated in the eighteenth century. The large, solid, stylized trees were first painted in a deep dark green, then overlaid with a simple pattern of leaves and tiny flowers (*see detail, below left*). As a background, exquisitely painted birds have been plucked from their resting places in the trees, to sit and preen themselves as they float unperturbed in the air, counterbalancing the heaviness of the trees. The border of red, green and yellow picks out the main colours of the panel and brings the composition together. Inside work such as this was done over dry plaster made from marble dust and lime, which was then polished with an agate stone so it was very smooth with a soft sheen. It was painted using a plant gum or resin mixed with pigments.

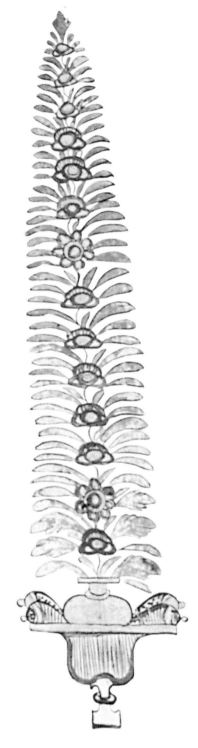

DU HVAD:VAR

FRUITS AND FLOWERS

A symmetrical lily plant has become almost abstract, perfectly filling the shape between the door and cupboard in Carl Larsson's house at Sundborn, Sweden, painted from about 1903. The wall designs are worked in almost flat paint, outlined in black. The equally symmetrical but more loosely painted design on the door is a reworking of traditional motifs. The little portrait on the door has been adorned and framed by garlands, ribbons and bows, rather in the manner of an eighteenth-century print room. The colours echo the rest of the decorations – the pale pink is the orange with a lot of white added. The particular green and orange of the woodwork, with white on the door and surround, have become almost synonymous with this painter. The painted-glass windows of the cupboard depict the artist with his wife, Karin.

FRUITS AND FLOWERS

The landscapes on the four panels of this cupboard from Cortina d'Ampezzo in the Italian Dolomites were painted in 1767. Leafy scenes such as these are not particularly common, as they require a little more skill. In fact, the paintwork is quite economical, possibly a sponge was used to make the leafy tops of trees – see the three trees in the detail (*below*). Around the panels, scrollwork is painted in ochre, in imitation of baroque plasterwork or carving. The bell flowers are loosely executed and hang at a rakish angle.

This delightful arrangement of flowers in a vase is set in a painted fireplace and tiled surround on an English *trompe l'oeil* chimney board. These wooden boards were used to cover fireplaces during the summer months to protect the room from draughts and falling soot. This particular example, dating from 1730, was painted in oils. Over time, some of the leaves have turned blue because of the use of a fugitive yellow pigment (confusingly called Dutch pink) which, in fading, has left only the Prussian blue remaining. The work on the tiles (*see detail, left*) shows a very practised hand – just a few confident brush strokes make up the picture. To separate each tile, a line has been incised, which is usually done by making a furrow in the still wet paint using a brush end. Note how the architectural detail is done so simply and superbly, using only three tones of brown.

FRUITS AND FLOWERS

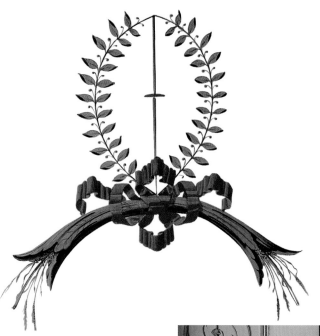

The walls of the Boudoir at Attingham Park, Shropshire, England, were painted in 1785 in the classical style, probably using oil paint. They have been attributed to the French artist Louis Delabrière. Unless you are a talented artist yourself, work like this serves as a lesson in colour and balance. Earthy terracotta pink and greyed green leaves, tinged with pink, elegantly swirl down the slightly umbered white wall. The balance between fine and broadening lines as well as horizontal and vertical shapes is superb.

The leaf design (*see detail, left*) is seen on all manner of walls and furniture in different guises. The method of painting it is simple, involving one tone for the leaf and a darker tone of the same colour for the shadow. The convention is to imagine that the light is falling from above left. The leaves, tied by a classic red ribbon, are clustered together to form a type of cornucopia with dainty grasses and leaves emerging.

This leafy border with oranges and blossoms (*left*) was done in fresco on the wall of the Schloss Charlottenhof in Potsdam, Germany, in 1820 under the direction of the architect Karl Friedrich Schinkel. A favourite classical idea is to make a border from solid leaves, adding flowers or fruit for colour and shape. Although sometimes the borders are straight, more usually they are swagged or wreathed.

Foliage painted as if twisted around a pole has long been a popular way to decorate bedposts or chair legs. On a bed in Shelburne, Vermont, USA, delicate leaves, tiny grapes and fuchsias wind their way around an ivory-painted bedpost (*far right*). The painting makes them seem to grow from the base, starting large then becoming progressively smaller and finer as they approach the top.

A more formal interpretation of the same idea can be seen on a bedpost (*near right*) of a bed that is part of a set of furniture at Castle Howard, in Yorkshire, England, decorated by John Linnell in the late eighteenth century. The beautiful golden-coloured wood is a satinwood called fustic. Here, the leaves are regular, staying the same size and more or less the same distance apart. At the base, long thin leaf shapes hang down and hug the post. If you are attempting this design, work out the position of the twisting vine by wrapping a piece of string around the post and marking its position in pencil.

FRUITS AND FLOWERS

The rows of perfectly painted dots around this Swiss chest give it a lively, impromptu look. Originally, the base must have been a pale green but age has worn most of it away so all that remains is the wood. The vases of flowers and the decorations used on the panels are symmetrical but each side is not exactly the same, indicating that although stencils may have been used to create the overall shape, considerable hand-painting must also have been done.

To achieve this uneven paintwork, use wax on some areas. (If the wood is new, it may be necessary to seal it first so the wax does not soak into the wood too much.) Apply the wax in irregular patches by melting it slightly so it can be painted on or by rubbing soft wax on with a stiff brush. When the wax has set, stencil or hand-paint the design – the areas with the wax will not allow the paint to adhere. When dry, rub over the work gently with steel wool, which will remove the wax.

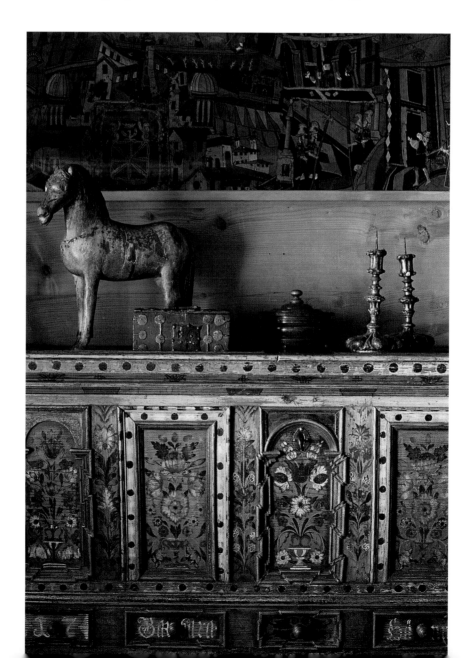

FRUITS AND
FLOWERS

A beautifully painted basket of flowers provides a central focus on this bureau-cabinet (*right*) from northern Italy. It is perched on red-painted stylized foliage shapes which initially were copies of plasterwork. To give the foliage a three-dimensional look, the basic shape is painted in a mid-red and then highlighted with a soft pink and shaded with a darker red. A long, flowering stem is entwined around the upper scrollwork of the lid.

The colours in the stencilled decoration on this Early American rocking chair (*left*) have faded to variations of brown, from warm reds to ochres and deep umbers. Both the design and the colours are reminiscent of early Dutch marquetry. The method of stencilling used here involves making the edges very dark, which helps to give the shapes depth. To define the stems or veins and to outline some of the flower petals, very fine lines have been hand-painted.

FRUITS AND FLOWERS

Vanessa Bell painted this eighteenth-century bed (*below*) at Charleston, East Sussex, England, in the 1950s with an inventive decoration. A night scene, it shows two lit candles either side of a dressing table mirror which reflects some tulips. In front of the mirror lies a posy of flowers. The painted curtains help to make the long rectangle a better shape to work with.

The walls and cupboard (*right*) are the work of Eric Eliasson, a painter from Rättvik, Sweden, and were painted in about 1781. The scenes on the walls are from the Bible but, judging by the clothes and style, are set very definitely in eighteenth-century Sweden. On the panels the enormous stylized flowers are the size of trees and match those on the cupboard.

FRUITS AND
FLOWERS

These exuberant, happy and outrageously painted pieces of furniture were done in Hungary in the nineteenth century in small village joinery workshops. The two below are coverings for a recess in a wall with a door in the centre, while the dresser (*opposite*) is a freestanding piece of furniture. Dates and names were often included to commemorate either a wedding or some other anniversary. The paint is egg tempera, which explains the brightness and intensity of the colours. Pigment is mixed with the yolk of an egg and a little water, resulting in a very strong, slightly shiny surface. The red and white of the flowers sing out against the dark backgrounds of green, blue and brown. All the designs are of a similar size and evenly distributed, so no particular aspect overpowers. Everything is very simply hand-painted, mainly using dots, spots, circles and lines.

A similar effect could be achieved using stencils. Apply a very small amount of paint to a stencil brush, and then, rather than pouncing or stippling with the brush, instead brush the bristles to the side as you would a normal paint brush, thus giving the paint a wiped look. This can be emphasized by strengthening some areas with a second application of paint to create a thick, textured look when the stencil has been removed. For the pinkish-red shade, which is the colour of red earth, use a pale red oxide rather than a modern bright red, which could look too harsh. Off-white, ochre and cream can also be used on dark green and warm brown bases.

FRUITS AND
FLOWERS

Pen-and-ink has been used to make the designs on the tea caddy (*below*) and the border from a Regency sewing box (*above*). Penwork was a technique that was used towards the end of the eighteenth and beginning of the nineteenth century, when it was popular as an amusement for ladies of leisure. Some examples were worked directly on to ivory, others on to wood and still others, like these, on to a white-painted base, all using a nib pen and black ink. The motifs were often flowers and leaves, and suggest marquetry as well as Oriental designs.

This Sheraton-style secretaire (*opposite*) in the Drawing Room at Fenton House, Hampstead, London, is dated 1790 but the hand-painted decoration on the drawer and bureau front was probably done later, possibly in the nineteenth century. The beautiful honeyed tones and the smooth rippling grain of the satinwood work well with decorative painting. A trail of leaves and flowers makes its way gently around the bureau front, creating a border. It has been painted in white and shaded in umber so that the eye focuses on the soft colours of the early summer blossoms above and below it. The colours are generally pale with the exception of the deep green behind the central roses, which helps to give a greater sense of depth and makes the whole bouquet seem to float.

When Francesco Davizzi and Catelana degli Alberti
married in 1395, the rooms of their grand Florentine
house, the Palazzo Davanzati, were painted in the most
elaborate and arresting way. On the walls of this room
(*opposite*), like many of the others in the palace, a *trompe
l'oeil* trick has been used. Wall hangings have been painted
that have a repeated, complex geometric pattern with
heraldic motifs. Near a door into a small ante-room, the
"hanging" is caught back to reveal that its "lining" is
miniver, the winter pelts of squirrels, suggesting opulence
and warmth. Beneath the hanging is revealed a delightful
garden of simple flowering trees, with the leaves and
flowers like dots against the dark green background.
Through the archway, in the room probably used for
bathing, a breathtakingly simple design of flowers is
painted. Although at first the flowers all look the same,
each is subtly different from the rest.

On the walls of a stately
house in Goa, a stencilled
design echoes both the
open-trellised ceiling and
the tiled floor (*left*). The
design is very regular
and repetitive, with the
flower repeated on every
second square.

Figures and animals

In this section there is a huge variety of styles and designs. The most frequently painted animals in decorative painting are probably birds, as they lend themselves so well to pattern making, but horses and elephants are also very decorative, especially when painted in the Indian style.

Painting people and animals on furniture or walls can be difficult for a decorative painter, who has to decide whether the figure is to be naturalistic or stylized. Naturalistic figures can be quite a challenge. The beautifully painted horse on page 66 is not possible for everybody. To stylize a figure it must be simplified. Folk painters do this beautifully, as is particularly apparent in some Swedish rooms. Perhaps the best examples of stylized work that is not naïve are chinoiserie-painted furniture, in which the figures are stylized yet extremely elegant.

Two beautifully dressed soldiers try to look fierce while guarding the entrance to a room in this Swedish interior decorated in the eighteenth century. Life-size figures, often freestanding cut-outs, were popular additions to rooms at that time. The doors, archway and faux columns have been marbled, demonstrating the importance of the building.

FIGURES AND
ANIMALS

These cupboard doors (*below*), painted by Myro Gorsky for a house in Tuscany, Italy, have delightful classical figures painted within roundels and landscapes painted within lozenges. The decorative effect of the patterns is enhanced by the stronger blue behind the figures (see *detail, below left*). The two rope patterns work together to make a powerful chevron shape in the centre of the cupboard.

At Crathes Castle in Scotland, this ceiling painted in the sixteenth-century (*opposite*) depicting the Muses shows women playing musical instruments and also includes classical motifs. Painting on the ceiling in this style was a form of decoration that was fairly widespread in Scotland as a result of trading links with Scandinavia. It was probably executed by an itinerant painter and decorator who used pattern books for the design. The work was done using glue size as the medium, with pigment to colour it. On the undersides of the beams simple abstract designs have been painted, while on the sides pious tracts and poems are written.

FIGURES AND ANIMALS

Bible stories have been a popular theme for furniture and wall decoration. On a wall in a Swedish bedroom, scenes from a story are individually framed. In one frame of the story (*opposite*), two holy figures with shining haloes talk to a woman in a decidedly Swedish landscape. The artist has tried to make the picture naturalistic although there is a certain amount of stylization in the trees.

The chest of drawers (*right*) has been painted more with the intention of creating patterns. Boldly coloured angels stand symmetrically by the side of the simplified tulip plant which, in an imaginative touch, holds the key plate (*see detail, below*). There is a number of small decorative motifs around the chest and an interesting star shape on the side. The chest, from Pennsylvania, USA, was painted in 1835.

In Sweden it was customary in the eighteenth century to have one room in the house that was used for entertaining and for celebrating important days in the Christian calendar as well as birthdays, weddings, christenings and deaths. Scenes from the Bible and "improving" stories would be painted on the walls using templates from pattern books to make the designs. On the walls of this room (*left*) the same face is used for each figure.

This oak wood settle (*left*) can be seen at Wightwick Manor, a house with decoration by William Morris, in Staffordshire, England. The panels were painted in oils during the late nineteenth century by Charles Eamer Kempe, a stained glass artist. They depict the four seasons (see *detail, above*), a popular theme of the time.

FIGURES AND ANIMALS

The scenes on this richly decorated bureau-cabinet are simply coloured prints pasted on to a painted background and framed with paper borders. It is reminiscent of the eighteenth-century print room, in which the same method of decoration was used on walls. The cabinet is eighteenth-century Venetian. Painted furniture had by then become so popular that hand-painted pieces couldn't be done fast enough to keep up with demand, and so paper cut-outs began to be used. When this type of work is of Italian origin, it is usually called *lacca povera* rather than découpage. The yellowness of the work was probably the result of applying an oil varnish to protect and enhance the prints.

Here we have two eighteenth-century chinoiserie cabinets with quite different characters. The English, green lacquer cabinet (*opposite*) has Chinese figures arranged like ladies and gentlemen in a garden setting, in the European manner, with a line of classical bell flowers down the edge. Only the motifs at the front, such as the ship, the ducks (see *detail, opposite top*) and the bridge (see *detail, opposite below*), are not in perspective. The designs here are very fine. For a similar effect you could use bronze powders and then varnish well.

The red lacquer cabinet (*left*), decorated in Spain in the Chinese style, has many small individual designs all over it, each one quite separate from the others. Although the figures are Chinese, the motifs have a decidedly European look about them, making them highly decorative in a naïve way. The work is delightfully coloured in white and blue, giving it an unusual effect.

Paper cut-outs decorate this pretty Venetian bureau-cabinet from the eighteenth century. Over a white and pale blue painted background, red decorative frames divide up the doors and drawer fronts into more manageable areas. Prints of rural scenes are coloured very delicately with watercolours and pasted down, connected each time to the edge of the frame in some way to give them a little solidity. In the corners and along the edges there are very small figures and some small floral motifs.

FIGURES AND ANIMALS

Only the front remains of this Italian chest, called a *cassone*, in which a bride carried her dowry. The panels of many such chests have been removed and treated as framed paintings. A long, thin shape like this is awkward to decorate, so the solution was often to create a central motif – here a fountain, but sometimes a table full of food – with similar scenes on either side. This *cassone*, painted by Giovanni Toscani (1370–1430), is titled "The Garden of Love".

FIGURES AND ANIMALS

Birds are a very popular motif with which to decorate as they come in so many shapes and colours. A homely chicken (*below*) guards her little chicks on the nursery frieze at Wightwick Manor, in Staffordshire, England. The frieze was stencilled and hand-painted by Cecil Aldin in 1910. The lengths of the paper frieze could be bought ready-decorated, to be pasted directly on the wall.

The Mexican decorations on this sideboard (*above*) are brilliant in their wildly decorated plumage and exotic colouring.

Painted in oil on linen, the Chinese rooster on his mound (*near right*) provides an elegant and restrained decoration on the walls of Regnaholm, in Sweden.

This exquisitely painted hoopoe bird (*far right, top*) is from the background of the decorations at the eighteenth-century Samode Palace in Rajasthan, India. The colours are natural and lifelike, but the slightly flattened profile and patterning are a little stylized.

At the Château d'Anet in northern France, a large pair of doors was decorated in the eighteenth century with classical motifs forming panels. On the larger panel (*below*) two winged sphinxes hold a wreath for a very naturalistically painted bird of prey, caught at the moment of the kill. Below this (*bottom*), in a quieter mood, sit two demure rabbits in roundels between classical wreaths making up a border.

FIGURES AND ANIMALS

FIGURES AND ANIMALS

The familiar structure of three archways has been used on this eighteenth-century blanket chest (*above and below*) from Pennsylvania, USA. In the centre, two awkward-looking symmetrical horses stand either side of a tree, like heraldic lions. A design like this could have been done with plain, coloured paper folded in half: after the design was cut out of it, the paper was unfolded then pasted down on the painted background, creating rather crude, chunky shapes.

The technique used for these elephants (*opposite*), dating from 1890, was similar to those of Italian frescos. Outside work, like this on a staircase in a courtyard of an *haveli* in Mandawa, Rajasthan, India, was painted into wet plaster with details applied later when dry. The plaster was made of lime, marble dust or powdered shells and milk curds, so the finished surface could be burnished, or given a gloss with coconut oil. Later overpainting may have caused the flaking paint.

FIGURES AND ANIMALS

This stately horse (*right, and below*) stands on a plinth decorated with a classical trophy motif on the doors of a room in the Château d'Anet in northern France. His setting is cool, classical and sparsely decorated. On his back is a blanket with heraldic motifs and a decorative golden chain.

On a vaulted ceiling (*above*) in the Sigtia
Haveli, Rajasthan, India, decorated in the
nineteenth century, horses, elephants,
camels, a dog, a monkey and even a
peacock form a busy and richly patterned
procession. The idea with this type of
decoration is to fill the space, so where
there is a gap, a dog or bird is painted
with no concern for size or perspective.
Each horse, like many other elements, is
exactly the same, so a stencil or template
must have been used and then filled in
with different colours. Few of the designs
overlap each other but they do just
touch, giving a feeling of fullness and
making interesting shapes with the design.

Classical

Some of the most beautiful classically painted furniture was done in the seventeenth and eighteenth centuries when decorators and furniture makers were stimulated by the classical world of ancient Greece and Rome. In France, Britain and Italy, particularly Venice, the art of painting furniture flourished. New colours – Prussian blue and greens, and clearer yellows and reds – and new materials, like the European lacquer shellac, became available. Architects such as the Adam brothers in Britain and Schinkel in Germany introduced painted decoration and classical motifs into their work following the excavations of Pompeii and Herculaneum in the 1740s. Scandinavia, which had a long tradition of painting furniture, incorporated the new classical ideas with enthusiasm. Since then, some of the motifs, such as the urn, ram's head and sphinx, have remained linked with classicism, but others, including swags, garlands, laurel wreaths, bell flowers and ribbons, have become widely popular.

One of the finest print rooms still in existence is the one at Castletown in County Kildare, Ireland. The decoration, by Lady Louisa Conolly, was started in 1762, but wasn't finished until possibly ten years after that. The large walls of the room were tackled in sections – one above the fireplace, one over the door and so on. Each section is beautifully balanced and symmetrical. As was the custom with print rooms, the prints were pasted directly onto the wall with paper borders around them and a mixture of paper garlands, trophies, chains and ribbons interspersed between them.

CLASSICAL

The rather heavy shape of this card table (*below*), made and decorated in Baltimore, Maryland, USA, in 1815, has been made to look lighter and more elegant by being grained and gilded with classical motifs. The central motif, repeated several times, is the palmetto, a stylized palm-like design. Acanthus leaves, cornucopias and rosettes are also used. Three stages were involved in achieving this look, with a layer of varnish applied after each stage. For the first stage, a very dark brown glaze was applied over a slightly pinkish base coat and simply dragged to make a coarse-grained mahogany effect. Over this, gilded designs were worked, probably using bronze powders. Finally all the delicate work painting the fruits and veins of the leaves was done using a fine brush and brown paint.

This magnificent bed in Lady Georgiana's bedroom (*below*) at Castle Howard in Yorkshire, England, dating from about 1780, has a beautifully painted shaped canopy. The pelmet over the window is similarly treated. On the dark claret moulding, white plumes are interspersed with golden-ochre rosettes. Below this, green leaf shapes appear to hang, with a white diamond shape between them. On the diamond is a small classic flower. The edging of blue helps to bring these classic colours to life.

John Linnell was commissioned in the late eighteenth century to paint a suite of furniture for this bedroom at Castle Howard in Yorkshire, England. It consisted of the bed, eight chairs, two pelmets (cornices) and two bedside cabinets, all decorated in tones of classic green over a warm Brazilian satinwood called fustic. The other painted pieces in the room were added later. The chair backs (see *detail, below*) have a feather motif, with the popular bell flower motif below descreasing in size to become small spheres. There are also acanthus leaves and crossed palm leaves as well as leaf shapes that echo those on the bed's canopy and bedpost.

CLASSICAL

London's Osterley Park, reconstructed by Robert Adam in the eighteenth century, was one of his greatest triumphs. Inspired by the ancient classical world, he designed the Etruscan Room between 1760 and 1780, using many of his favourite motifs in the room. The wall decoration was painted by Pietro Maria Borgnis, on sheets of paper pasted on to canvas and fixed to the walls.

The urn (*below left*), mounted on a stand decorated with ram's heads, was one of Adam's favourite motifs. On the door panels the motifs are exquisitely balanced between small grisaille medallions and delicate drops of bell flowers.

The Etruscan Room is very high, so around the room at the same height as the pelmet above the door is a small border, from which swagged beads and medallions hang on ribbons. Two nymphs (*left*) stand coyly on either side of an urn containing delicate garlands of flowers. Everywhere the same motifs recur in different guises, particularly the honeysuckle, husk or bell flower, medallion, swag and oval patera.

CLASSICAL

The introduction of a well-placed line on a wall or painted decoration can be the foundation of a work. Sometimes the decoration can consist almost entirely of lines. In a room (*opposite*) at Skansen, Sweden, the decoration of the wall is an elaborate frame in a soft yellowish pink with greys; there is nothing in the frame except a classical arrangement of acanthus leaves and balls. The *trompe l'oeil* border conforms to the usual convention of suggesting that the light comes from above left. The decoration was done on stretched canvas and applied to the walls with an actual piece of moulding around the edges.

This painted corner decoration (*right, above*) was done in the nineteenth century in a house in London. Three black lines make up the outer border but the inner border is more complex, with a very elaborate corner piece. The *trompe l'oeil* moulding sprouts leaves and flowers which twist their way around a central rosette.

Similar to the Swedish decoration opposite, this design (*right, below*) uses red and yellow on an off-white wall to represent moulding.

CLASSICAL

Chair legs can be a problem to decorate as they have such a small surface area. Painting simple lines is often an easy solution. On this chair painted with pale yellow ochre (*right*), lines have been incised at regular intervals to resemble bamboo, and then filled with black paint, making a simple decoration. The seat has been delineated with a black painted line around the outer edge; a reddish-brown line on the seat edge connects by colour to the chair back. The rest is left unpainted.

On this dun-coloured chair (*left*) decorated in the nineteenth century, three simple lines follow the shape of the chair back.

An American dressing table, painted in 1835, has fine black lines following the shape of the back and delineating the drawer fronts and legs. Many people are daunted by the prospect of painting lines but one look at these charmingly uneven ones proves that they do not have to be perfect to be successful.

Bell flowers, or oat husks as they are sometimes called, are seen in one form or another on almost every painted piece of decoration in the eighteenth century. Here (*left*) they form the edge of some chinoiserie decoration.

This simple bedroom chair (*right*) was painted in just two colours. A fan shape in the oval with the central medallion was a typical design.

In the eighteenth century some chairs were designed to be painted – without the paint the design looked odd. This very fine George III chair (*left*) was wood-grained and then painted with an urn, garlands, ribbons and leaves as well as the ubiquitous bell flowers, in green and terracotta.

This chair at Osterley Park in London (*left*) has a back shaped like an urn, one of Adam's favourite motifs. This was then painted with medallions and bell flowers to match the decoration on the walls.

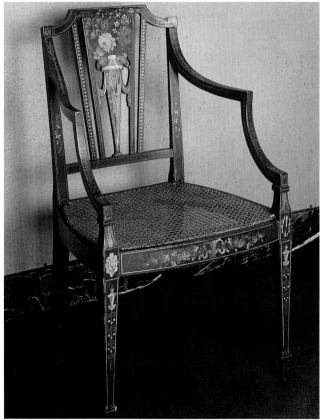

A chair (*left*) painted in 1750 for a bedroom is decorated with a tall flower vase from which drapes hang. This is edged with two splats on either side of a row of balls or buttons (see *detail, right*), a popular border design.

The colours and design used on the wall of this Finnish interior have a magical, theatrical quality. The three-dimensional moulding has been painstakingly picked out and the stars gilded in metallic leaf. A neat little swag of fabric hangs below the border of alternate panels of sphinxes and swans.

Strapwork designs are flat, ribbon-like bands interlaced and folded into decorative patterns, rather like designs used in Celtic knots and heraldic chains. The bands are often interspersed with circles or oval holes. Strapwork, which is thought to have developed from Islamic metalwork design, became popular in the sixteenth and seventeeth centuries in northern Europe.

The decoration on this ceiling (*above*) in Hävinge Castle, Sweden, has an outer band of strapwork in a light stone colour on a warm pink base. The design is made up of two pairs of "ribbons" twisted together in an open plait.

The spectacular strapwork decoration on the Great Staircase (*opposite*) at Knole, in Kent, England, is thought to have been carried out in 1627 by Paul Isaacson, a master painter and stainer. The painting, done in a series of pale browns, off-white, greys and sienna yellows, includes certain aspects of classical design in rather restrained form, such as bowls of fruit, acanthus leaves and even a solitary bell flower on the panel underneath the stairs. The painted balustrade on the wall is an unusually early example of *trompe l'oeil*.

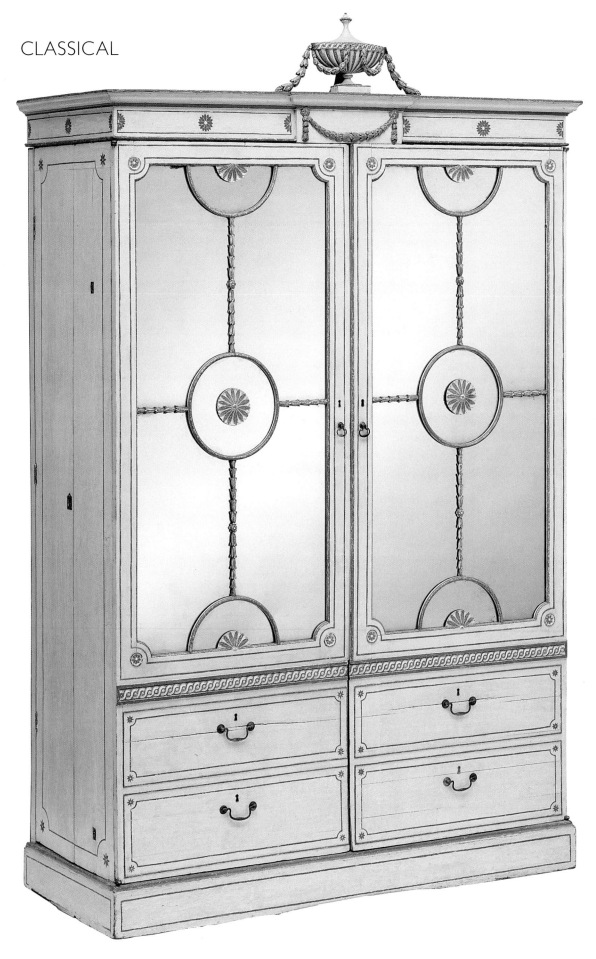

This cabinet (*opposite*), which contains a foldaway bed, was made in 1768 by Thomas Chippendale for the actor–manager David Garrick, as part of a suite of furniture for his house at Twickenham, England. The green and cream are classic eighteenth-century colours. Here the green has been applied not only to the moulded and carved areas but also to make lines and rosettes that copy the carved rosettes, adding interest to an otherwise relatively simple piece of furniture.

This George III semicircular giltwood side table (*below*) has a front of gilded wood and a partly painted white marble top (*right*). This was a popular eighteenth-century piece of furniture, offering an interesting shape to decorate. Often a fan shape was painted on a semicircular table, but here the shape of the table has been emphasized with a band at the edge and a central semicircle. In the two bands on the cool blue-grey background there is a repeated pattern of classical urns linked with anthemions and scrolling foliage. In the semicircle are rather large, frilly, warm-coloured acanthus leaves and slim long leaves, making a necklace-shaped focus for the table.

The Royal Pavilion in Brighton, England, is where eastern design meets western with a loud fanfare. The building was designed by John Nash for the Prince Regent in an extravagant and exotic style. On the outside it looks like an Indian palace, but the inside is heavily influenced by Chinese decoration. All of the decorative painting and gilding was carried out by Robert Jones and the Crace brothers in the early 1820s. In the entrance hall (*left*) a *trompe l'oeil* Chinese lattice-work design has been painted in oils and surmounted by classical acanthus leaves and an acorn.

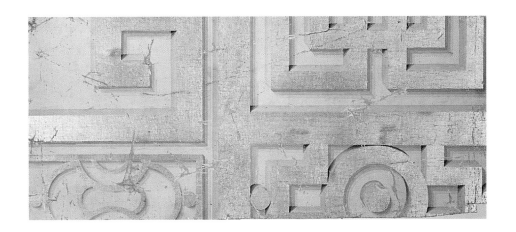

In the Music Room Gallery (*above*) the walls have been given
a very delicate *trompe l'oeil* Chinese lattice-work effect using
18-carat gold leaf and paint in greys and cream, with
terracotta red in the shadows. In the South Gallery (*below*)
the doors have been wood-grained and lattice-work borders
have been added in blue. On the blue pillars either side of
the door is an enlargement of a design usually found in tiny
sections in porcelain or lacquerwork. On the wall there is a
soft matt blue distemper, with a lattice-work design in paper
cut out and pasted on to the blue background.

CLASSICAL

This extraordinarily rich and elaborate room was originally in the Château de la Tournerie, near Le Mans in north-western France. Who did it or exactly whom it was for is not known. However, the intertwined monogrammed initials on certain panels suggest that it was painted in the late seventeenth century for Alexander Sévin and his wife, Charlotte le Meusnier. The main part of the room, including the ceiling, is richly decorated with gold with painted decoration over it. This includes, in some form or another, practically every classical motif ever devised, as well as some heraldic motifs, such as the chequered backgrounds on some of the panels (below). There are cherubs, dolphins, eagles, cornucopias and masks as well as the more commonplace drapes, ribbons, garlands, rosettes and acanthus leaves. Some panels also depict popular mythological figures and legends such as Juno and the Peacock, Hercules and Prometheus. The large dark panel with flowers and birds is embossed and stamped as if it were Cordovan leather, a decorative material popular with the wealthy at that time. Above the fireplace is a conventional painting of the *Adoration of the Shepherds* which seems very plain in comparison with its surroundings.

Abstract and geometric

The words abstract and geometric conjure up something modern but, of course, designs which refer neither to the plant nor to the animal world have been produced since time immemorial. Dots, spots, lines, crosses, crescents, chevrons, circles, squares and triangles are patterns that are at the disposal of anybody, even the most untrained decorator. The difficult part is arranging these simple shapes in a pleasing design – but inspiration can be taken from sources such as patterns on china, embroidered samplers, tile designs and calligraphy pattern sheets, to name just a few.

This magnificent door with its *trompe l'oeil* panelling (*opposite*) comes at the end of a long corridor in Powis Castle, Wales, and has been in situ since 1593. Legend has it that it was brought from a local monastery and the rest of the room was decorated at a later date to match.

These beams (*below*) were painted at Culross Palace, Scotland, in the seventeenth century.

These remarkable rooms in a medieval castle, Nyborg Slot on the island of Fyn in Denmark, were once the chambers of the king and queen of Denmark. Decorated in the early sixteenth century with tremendous ingenuity, they use only three tones – black, grey and white. In the inner room, the King's Room (*opposite*), the design is simply four triangles making up a square. The decoration of the adjoining Queen's Chamber (*right, above*) is more elaborate and gives the walls a three-dimensional look. The use of the pattern from the King's Room in the window arch of the Queen's Chamber allows the two rooms to complement each other neatly. Note too the delightful hand-painted quality of these designs. No masking tape or spray guns were used, of course, and the measuring is sometimes a bit off, so the result is soft and mellow. The effect is best achieved through the rather laborious task of hand-painting, but something similar could be done more quickly by printing with sponges cut to shape, using a plumb line to keep everything straight.

ABSTRACT AND GEOMETRIC

The simple design and cheap pigments – red earth, white chalk and lamp black – of this chest (*below*) from Schoharie County, New York, USA, suggest that the owners had few resources at their disposal. Yet the effect is a fascinating patchwork design.

ABSTRACT AND GEOMETRIC

In the 1920s the Finnish painter Akseli Gallen-Kallela painted the decorations on this vaulted ceiling at Hvittrask (*opposite*), the home of the modernist architect Eliel Saarinen. The contrast between the flat, solid slate blue with small patches of shiny gold against the rough, concrete-like material gives this ceiling a delightful quality.

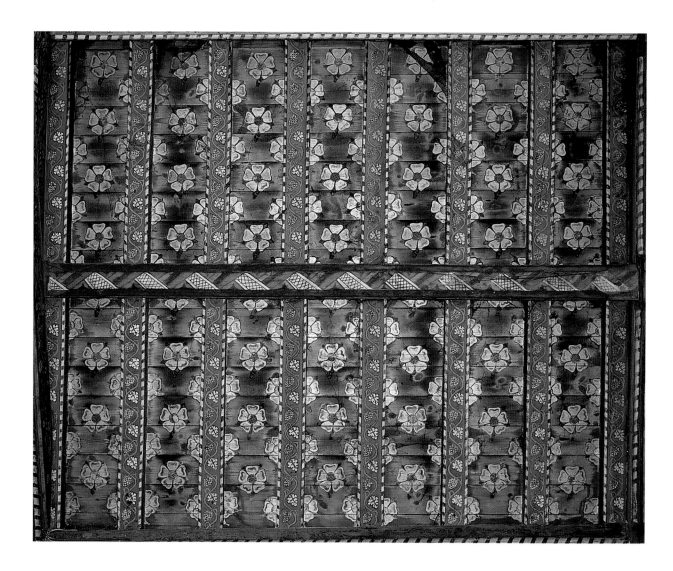

The ceiling (*above*) designed by William Morris for a church in Middleton Cheney, Northamptonshire, England, has a delightful arrangement of flower shapes which give a regular star-like pattern to the slats of the ceiling. Making an angular contrast, the central beam has an unusual pattern of folded zigzags in red, grey and white. The design is inspired by heraldic and medieval motifs, including the stripy edgings to the moulding.

ABSTRACT
AND
GEOMETRIC

At Charleston in East Sussex, England, Duncan Grant painted this corner cupboard (*opposite*) in 1925 with bold shapes and colours. On the tall, thin panels he probably started out thinking of columns but by simplifying the sections has ended up with a strong abstract idea. At the top of the "pillars" a capital has been scratched into the wet paint. The barleytwist columns at the sides have become a playful pattern in light and shade. The textured rag effect of the panels on the door, with the dark solid dots at the base, helps to balance the busy look of the painting above the panels.

A Hungarian shepherd's chest (*below*) dating from 1877 is painted in the dark green found almost all over the world on popular painted furniture of that time. The bright red paint would have been expensive then. To achieve a similar effect, distress a soft water-based paint by rubbing back with coarse steel wool or sandpaper using either wax or a patinating medium.

This bookcase (*opposite*) was originally decorated by Duncan Grant for a flat in Bloomsbury, London, in the early 1930s but came to Charleston in East Sussex with Clive Bell and is now in the library there. The designs are very simply painted over a white base and have the slightly contradictory look of being both spontaneous and thorough. Like designs on pottery, the decoration is done in one session rather than being overworked. The criss-crossed verticals, for instance, vary in colour as the paint runs out and the brush is recharged, so the result is lively and fresh. At the top of the cupboard on the brownish-red arches, the white scalloped line has been done by simply incising with a tool such as the end of a brush.

Inspired by bamboo, this delightful spotty chair (*right*) was done by Thomas Chippendale for the actor–manager David Garrick's house in Twickenham, England, in the eighteenth century. The chair was first painted in a white lacquer then divided into sections with black lines before the green spots were added. This was one way to make a simple country-style chair a little grander.

ABSTRACT
AND
GEOMETRIC

This cupboard (*below*) was designed by Charles Rennie Mackintosh around 1906 for his own house, several rooms of which have now been reconstructed in the Hunterian Art Gallery, Glasgow, Scotland. Although the design on the insides of the doors is based on a woman kissing a rose, the form has been so extended and elongated that it is easy to see it as an abstract decorative motif harmonizing with the pink oval heart shapes in the cupboard. The grey textured background offsets the hard black outline of the motif and softens the whole white-painted cabinet.

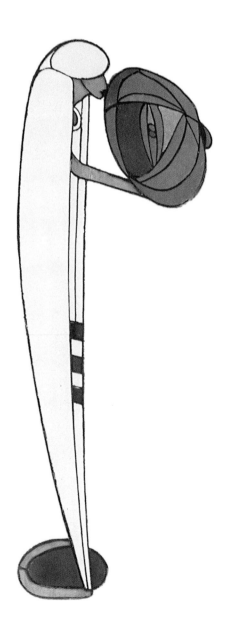

Charles Rennie Mackintosh's rigid and repetitive wall decoration (*above*) at Hill House in Scotland has been done using stencils. It has been executed carefully and cleanly so that the colour is very flat, even and without expression, although the colouring on the circular shape is not exactly the same each time. The design, in pinks and pale olive green, is based on roses but is so stylized that it has become hardly recognizable.

The circular geometric designs shown on these pieces are all forms of "hex" designs. Originating in Germany and Switzerland, these patterns were meant to ward off evil spells or bad luck (hex means witch or spell). There are many variations to the basic pattern. Other symbolism has also been brought in, and the star shapes could be said to come from a stylized pomegranate flower, representing prosperity and fertility.

This painted and decorated chest (*opposite*), dated 1824, comes from Pennsylvania, USA, and is typical of the style of painting known as Pennsylvania German (also sometimes called Pennsylvania Dutch). On the yellow background a brown glaze has been used, possibly in the form of vinegar painting, softening what would otherwise be a rather hard design. The rows of diamonds separating the sections (*see detail, opposite*) are reminiscent of ribbon designs.

ABSTRACT
AND
GEOMETRIC

The designs on this nineteenth-century Pennsylvanian blanket chest (*above*) are very clean and simple and are executed with neat care using very few colours. Perhaps the two hearts represent a bride and bridegroom.

In the study, called the Green Cabinet, at Rosersberg, the
summer retreat of the early nineteenth-century Swedish King
Karl XIII, the effect is warm and lively despite the hard lines
and strong colours and shapes. The walls have been decorated
as a simple print room, using coloured engravings and pasting
them directly on to the walls. The same border is used around
the prints as around the walls, unifying the treatment. Bold
hexagons and circles in imitation marble inlay have been
painted directly on to the floorboards, with the shapes echoed
by the circular motif on the cupboard doors. The texture of
the paintwork softens the whole effect, and the delightful
numbering on each cupboard gives a focus.

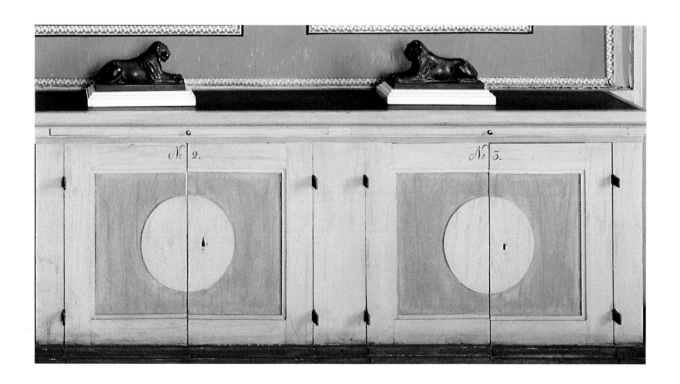

ABSTRACT
AND
GEOMETRIC

The design on this panel is the main motif to a set of bedroom furniture designed around the end of the nineteenth century in the Aesthetic style, which was popular at that time. The paintwork is in maroon, blue-grey and black worked directly on to the pinewood base. The decoration comes from a curious mixture of sources, resulting in an unusual design. The central and corner shapes are simplified eighteenth-century classical fan shapes, while the series of small lines on either side of the circle seems Chinese in inspiration and the rest is derived from a very formal Egyptian lotus design. When working straight on to wood in this way, it is necessary to rub down and seal the surface beforehand so that it is extremely smooth.

The scrolling paintwork on this corner cupboard from Hungary was inspired by a plant design. Instead of making it look naturalistic, the decorator has turned it into a dancing arabesque. At one time the green leaves were probably more apparent but they have since faded and now all that is left is a curling line running up each cupboard panel. The artist has made the most of the three colours by reversing the design on the panels.

ABSTRACT AND GEOMETRIC

This stunning and unusual chest of drawers was painted in Connecticut, USA, in the early eighteenth century. The decoration was probably applied using a stencil but a similar effect could be achieved by stamping, especially to obtain the blobby, uneven texture of the paint. The designs are made up out of just three patterns – a row of three crosses (in white), the dots (in red) and the motif resembling two back-to-back Es flanked by two dots (in red) – which are used on the side of the cupboard in a different formation.

The patterns on this chest with a drawer have been applied by both carving and colouring the wood with either paint or stain. At first sight, the decorations seem to be a number of arbitrary curved shapes cut into the wood, with a few scroll shapes scratched out here and there. Looking further, it is clear that the designs started out as floral folk decoration but, through the process of cutting and staining, other aspects of the patterns have been emphasized. Although the chest was painted in Connecticut, a similar style of work was found in parts of Switzerland, so the artist is likely to have come from there originally.

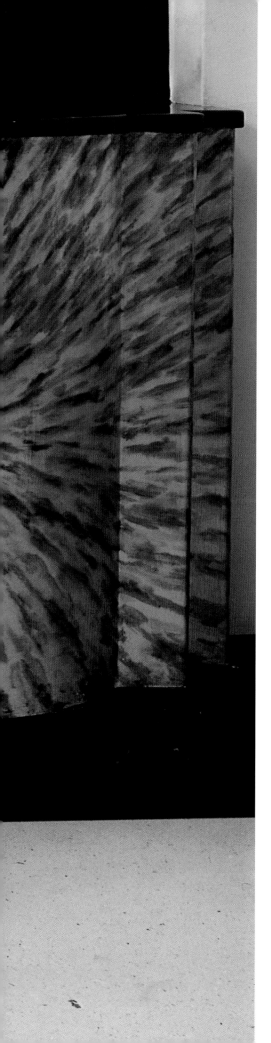

Finishes

The texture, and the textured look, of a surface are important to a wall or piece of furniture, giving subtle messages to the viewer about the decoration. The finish depends upon the type of paint used and the way it is applied. It can make the reflective quality of a surface, such as the glossy look of lacquerwork, indicate something new and fresh, or, at the other extreme, it can suggest the peaceful, mellow, matt look of distemper. The patina of years of use focuses our attention on the history of the painted item, adding another dimension to it. The finish can also indicate the use of transparent glazes as a basis for paint effects. Marbling and wood-graining are the backbone of paint finishes, and it is from these that many of the other techniques, such as stippling and combing, derive.

Every painted piece of decoration is defined by the type of brushwork used. A classical motif like an acanthus leaf may be painted very neatly, with sharp outlines, or it may be done so that the strokes of the brush are apparent, as in Duncan Grant's or Carl Larsson's work or in the flat style of the folk painter. Therefore, it is not simply the motif that must be considered but also the finish.

The foyer of Claridges Hotel, London, was decorated by Oswald Milne working with Basil Ionides in 1929, when glass, silver, lacquer, polished stones and exotic materials were all popular. Beneath an enormous tiled mirror, a panel of glistening tortoiseshell has been painted as a miniature of the similarly painted ceiling above. Next to this is the base of a silver-leaf and varnished pilaster for tall palm-shaped lights, and in front is the sleek shiny surface of a black lacquered sofa with gold-leaf lines.

Marbling became very popular as a paint effect in the late seventeenth century, when general interest in the revival of classical ideas began to emerge. It has retained its popularity ever since, in both naturalistic and decorative forms. At Attingham Park, Shropshire, England, the very naturalistic marbling in the entrance hall (*opposite*) was done under the direction of the architect John Nash in 1805. There is a main marble design covering most of the walls, as well as a darker border design around the grisaille pictures and doors and a third, even darker marble for the circular medallion shape and the arch around the fireplace. There are also grisaille panels. These are mostly by the same decorators as the marbling, but the one above the small door was by Robert Fagan, an Irish painter, dealer and diplomat.

At the Argory (*above*), a country house in County Tyrone, Northern Ireland, the walls of the West Hall were marbled at the turn of the nineteenth century. The paintwork continues all around the staircase.

FINISHES

The walls of the Chapel Drawing Room (*right*) at Belton House in Lincolnshire, England, were marbled in the late seventeenth century. When first painted, the faux marble was blue, but the effects of oil varnish and time have turned it green. Note that the marbled walls do not strive for reality by being divided into blocks, as they would have been in the eighteenth and nineteenth centuries. In the nineteenth century some other rooms in the house were marbled by the house painter George Sparrow.

The finish on this floor (*below*) is neither marble nor wood but an effect devised by Dutch farmers. The floor was painted with a pale brown colour and then a brownish transparent glaze was applied. While it was still wet, children would walk all over the floor in their bare feet, making oval and circular spots in the glaze. Often a stencilled border would be painted around the room also.

FINISHES

One type of marbling done particularly on folk-painted work in northern Europe in the eighteenth and nineteenth centuries was very decorative. The colours were often quite contrasting and the veining very exaggerated. Even objects that could never be made from marble were given this treatment, such as around the clock face and cornice of this grandfather clock (*below*) from Austria's Tyrol region. Decorated in 1735, it uses a base of white and red oxide with veins in a deeper brown.

The marbled panels in the door and cornice of this eighteenth-century Swedish house (*right*) are very decorative, becoming almost an abstract pattern. The matt floorboards are bleached, which was often done at that time using a mixture of soft soap and lye. The walls are covered with coarse linen painted by a Mr Schuffner; possibly the linen was varnished after being pasted on, which could account for the very yellow look of the surface.

The very stylish bathroom (*left*) at Beningbrough Hall in North Yorkshire, England, was decorated for Lady Chesterfield in the 1920s by Lenygon & Morant, a London firm of decorators. The marbling has been done on a black base, and the veins are painted in white with a little red oxide to pick up the colour of the stippled walls.

There are four very eccentric marbles, all in brown, painted on the walls of this Swedish house (*below*). All are worked over a diagonal base and then given stylized veining. The dado and column marbling has been made darker by using a dark brown for the veins. The blue-grey of the woodwork is effective in offsetting the powerful effect of the marbling.

FINISHES

A simple brushwork design has been used on the walls of this delightful Norwegian room. A sweep of the brush in a descending zigzag, using blue over white, gives an effect similar to that of lining the walls with fabric.

The texture of the
paintwork on the panels
and the surrounds gives
this work an immediacy
and a dynamic quality. The
door, at Charleston in East
Sussex, England, was
painted by Duncan Grant
in two stages: the vase of
flowers was done in 1917,
and the acrobat in 1958,
when the panel was
broken after playing
children accidentally
kicked it in.

FINISHES

In the Royal Pavilion at Brighton, England, decorated by Robert Jones and the Crace brothers in the early 1820s, faux bamboo was used in as many places as possible. Here it is seen on the Long Gallery staircase (*below left*), on a chair in the South Gallery (*below right*) and, inventively, on the skirting board in the Bow Rooms (*opposite*). Although it works best when the wood is shaped like bamboo, it can be successful even when painted on an ordinary pole. To suggest the bamboo, paint different-sized circles with a central dot and tapered lines using brown or black over yellow ochre.

On the door architrave in the Bow Rooms (*opposite*), an unusual technique was used to create an effect a little like an agate finish. Greys in various tones were applied and then combed at right angles to the grain of the wood using either a card or a comb wrapped in fabric to achieve a soft, lined finish. On the edge of the architrave and on the doors is satinwood graining.

FINISHES

Real gold leaf varies from pale watery yellow to a rich reddish tone, depending upon the amount of copper it contains. It is usually used over a base of an earth-red colour, which varies from a pinkish red to a dark orange. The gold used on this console table and frame (*right*) is dark and applied over a deep-coloured base.

This Venetian commode (*below*) has been parcel-gilded, meaning that only the carved areas have been gilded, in a light, bright gold. The warm terracotta bole base can be seen underneath the gold leaf. All this works perfectly with the old white paintwork and the yellow and pale terracotta flowers to make a very light, bright and pretty decorative finish.

The grey paint with the gold gives a cool look on this *Head of Bacchus* (*below*) in the Little Parlour at Uppark, West Sussex, England. Carved in about 1750, it was gilded in the nineteenth century.

FINISHES

These two very different pieces of furniture were both done in the eighteenth century, one (*below*) in the United States and the other (*right*) in Venice. An attractive patina has developed on both. On the simple American chest, few coats of paint were used so it has worn away quickly and the wood can be seen. On the Italian commode, there are more layers of paint and these have cracked and peeled off. The gilding has darkened or worn away completely, the blue has faded unevenly and some parts of the painted flowers have worn away. To create an antiqued, distressed effect similar to this, use a crackle medium between two coats of paint, followed by coarse steel wool or sandpaper to wear away the paint in patches, and then an antiquing medium in the form of a wax or specialist coat to darken and polish the finish.

Wood-graining is often an exacting art requiring the painter to imitate perfectly the delicate grain of a particular wood. It has been used for hundreds of years to simulate rare woods. On this English panelling from the 1600s (*left*), a very decorative and stylized wood has been painted in yellow and red, covering over the grey oak which at that time was commonplace and dull.

The bluish-grey and brown graining on horizontal planks (*below*) is an unusual idea in unusual colours but it works well. It is the original work done in Ayr Mount, North Carolina, USA, when it was first built in 1815. The brown glaze was probably hand-painted with the aid of combs for the close-grained edging. The small wooden chair has also been wood-grained but in dark, rich colours, and very subtly. Lines, borders and a classical honeysuckle pattern have been stencilled in bronze powders on the chair.

Motifs

How to use the motifs

This section contains eight pages of motifs, divided into each of the book's themes: Fruits and Flowers; Figures and Animals; Classical; and Abstract and Geometric. The designs chosen comprise a range of motifs that can be used together or separately to decorate furniture and walls. There are main motifs, small motifs and also designs that can be used as a complementary border. To enlarge them to the size needed for a particular project, use either a photocopier or a graphics program on a computer.

The designs are in tones of one colour so they can be used in different ways. A few suggestions have been included on which designs suit which technique.

Freehand painting

All the designs suit freehand painting in tones of one or more colours. A grisaille technique would be particularly effective with the classical themes. Begin by mixing three tones of the same colour – the dark and the light should be the same distance apart from the middle tone. It helps to look at the colours through half-closed eyes so all the details disappear and just the tones remain. Work at first only with the mid-tone and then fill in with the darker and finally the lighter tone. As you become more adept at this, more tones can be fitted in.

Try working with just three or four colours rather than a whole range, as the result can be too busy. With the folk paintings, remember to use traditional earth colours rather than very bright ones.

Gilding

The Chinese designs and some of the flower designs can be adapted well for gilding. Transfer the silhouette of the design onto the area you want to work with, then gild with leaf. Varnish, then paint the details with black or dark brown paint. Finish with a second layer of varnish.

Bronze powder can also be used – draw the design with gold size, following lines, dots and small areas, then lightly brush bronze powder in either one or two colours on to the size; complete with a coat of varnish. The finished effect is less bright than with the metal leaf.

Stencilling

Most designs can be turned into a stencil. Simplify them into medium-sized shapes, making "bridges" between each area. Very long shapes or very small or large shapes should be avoided. (To help you turn a design into a stencil, a griffin and a lion have been given in the Figures and Animals section of the motifs, and these show where bridges of the stencil have been made.) Some of the more complex flower designs can be finished off with hand-painting, or a second layer of stencil shapes can be made.

Stamping

Stamping is not really a traditional decorating technique except in fabric printing in the east and in Africa. This is because oil paints were mainly used, which do not print well, and also because the result is often uneven. Nowadays, when we are often after a textured, distressed effect full of character, stamping or other forms of block printing can work well. Potatoes, pieces of polystyrene, corks, sponges and even bits of thick cardboard make good surfaces to cut out and use.

Symbolic decoration   It can be amusing to choose decoration which has a particular meaning for you. The simple painted decoration of country folk relies not just on the colours and shapes but also on symbolic meanings. As chests and cupboards were often made to mark a wedding, appropriate symbols were needed and were applied rather like good-luck charms. Christian, classical and pagan symbols were freely combined.

Unicorns were guardians of virginity, doves were figures of peace and wedded bliss, and mermaids represented spirituality through the dual nature of Christ (half-human and half divine). Tulips were not only relatively easy to paint but also stood for wealth, spirituality and purity. The association with wealth derived from when tulipmania swept Europe in the seventeenth century and bulbs could cost a fortune. They were a symbol for spirituality because the three petals stood for the Holy Trinity, and a symbol for purity because a white tulip was like the white lily of the Virgin Mary. Fertility was symbolized by the tree of life, hearts and flowers; mating birds and Adam and Eve were also thought appropriate symbols. Other popular figures derived from classical mythology, particularly the Muses, the goddess of love and the goddess of hunting.

It is hard to identify with some of these meanings but others still seem potent and usable. It is perhaps time to invent some modern ideas, which could include symbols from other cultures such as African, Chinese, Native American and Aboriginal Australian. Use the motifs provided as starting blocks and then go on from there to find your own.

FRUITS AND
FLOWERS
MOTIFS

FIGURES AND ANIMALS MOTIFS

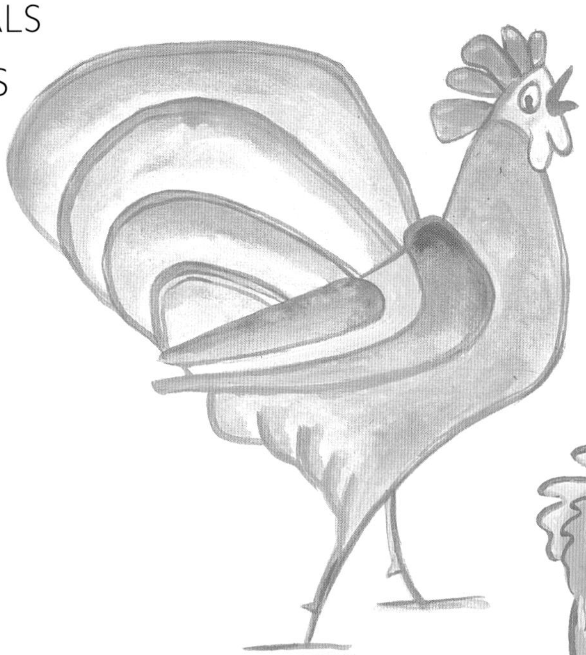

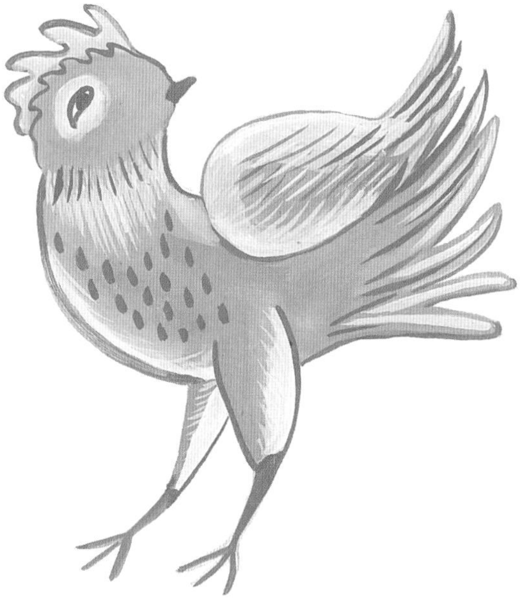

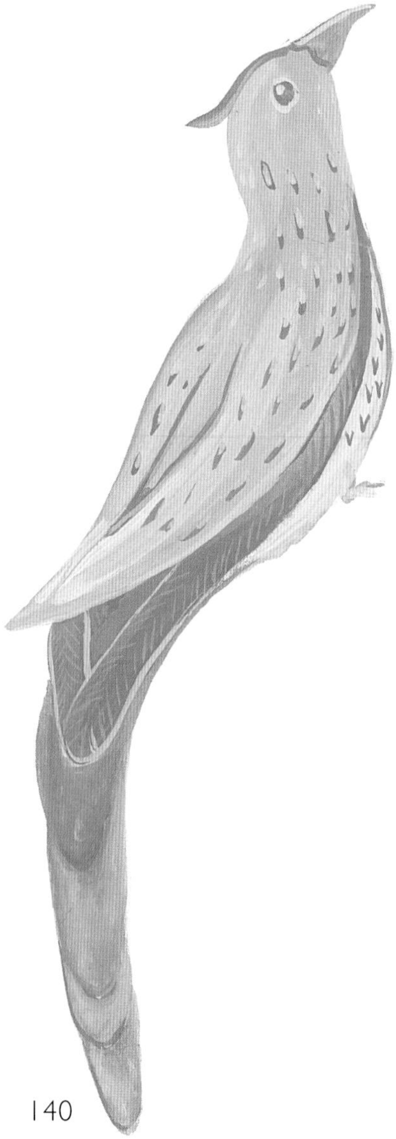

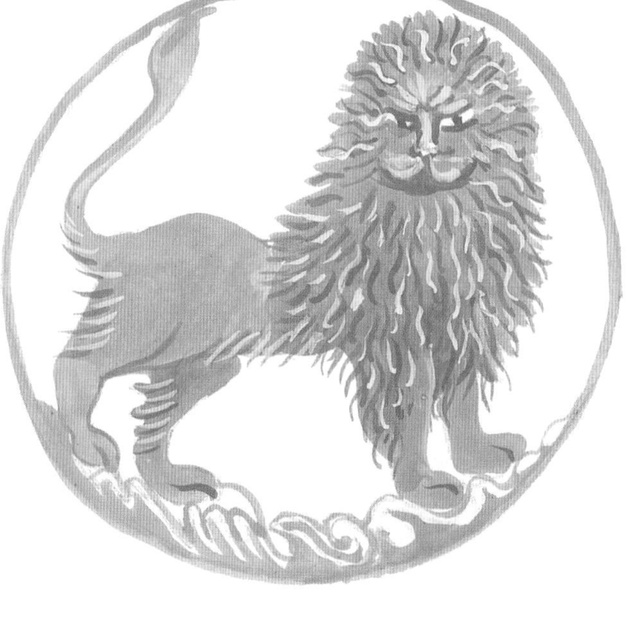

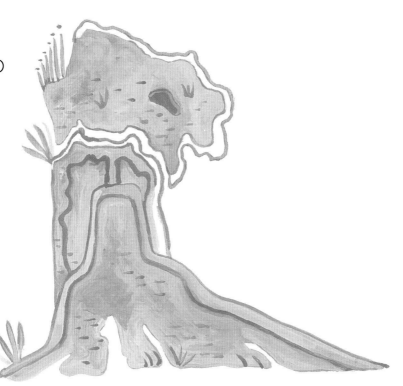

FIGURES AND ANIMALS MOTIFS

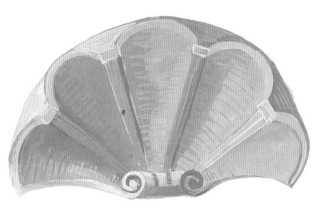

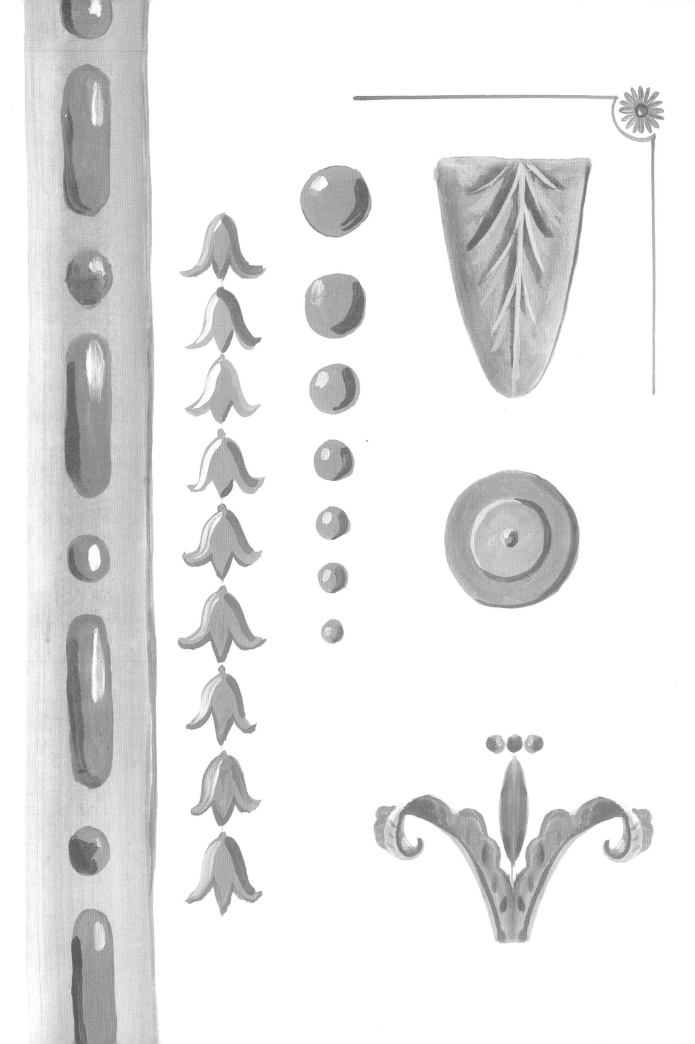

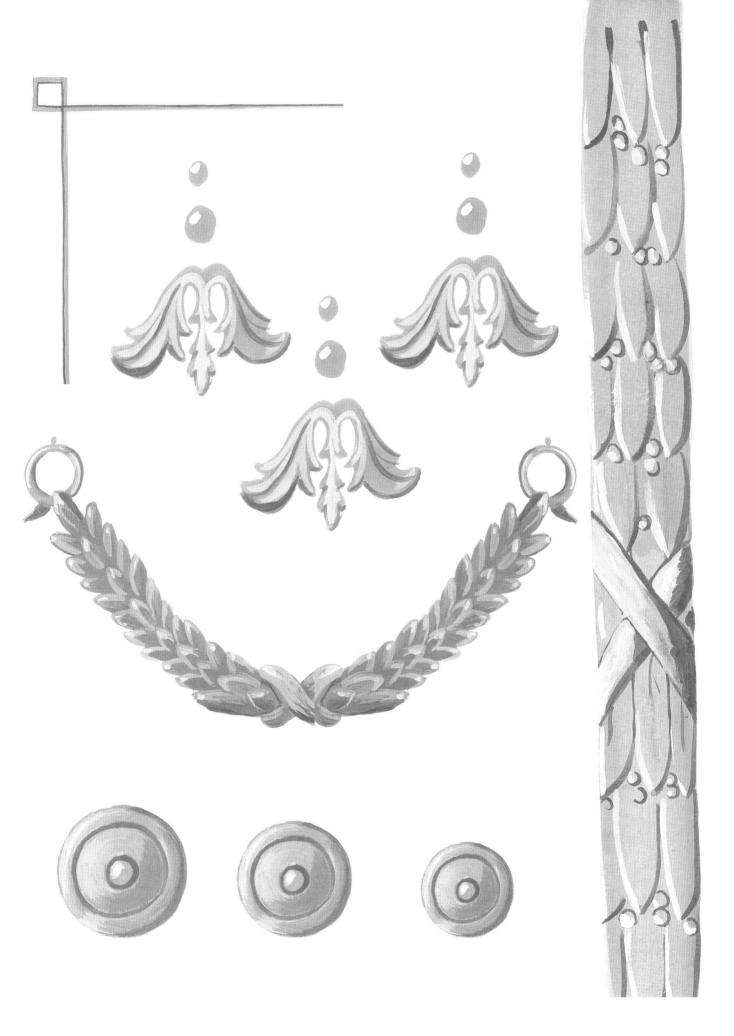

ABSTRACT AND GEOMETRIC MOTIFS

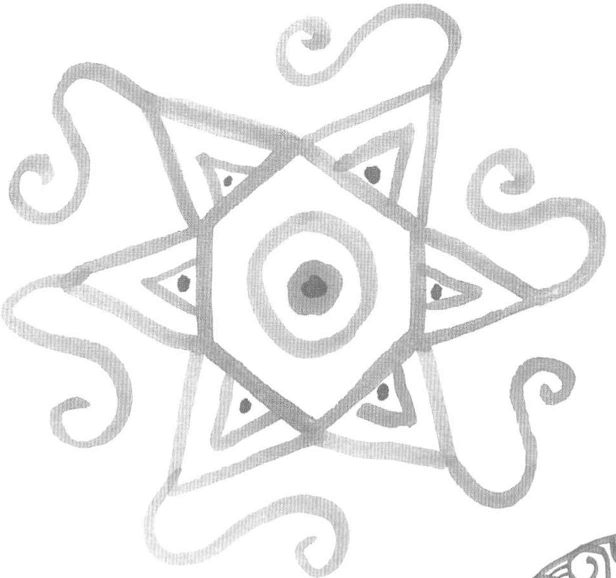

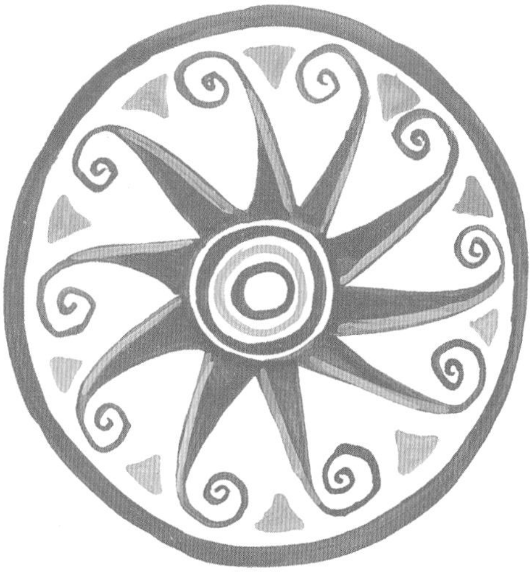

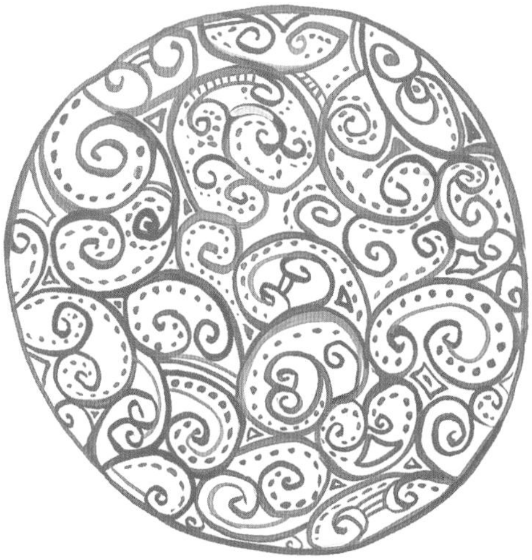

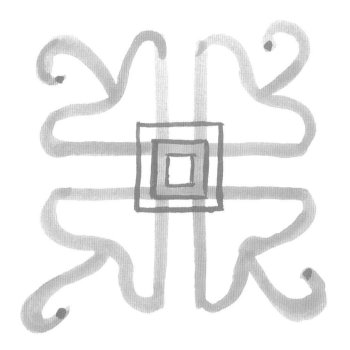

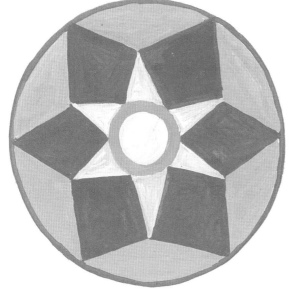

Glossary

Acanthus A classical motif based on the acanthus leaf. The basic design lends itself to many variations, including pointy; broad and bulbous; or long and delicate with tendrils and even thistle-like leaves.

Aged effect A paint effect that has the patina and appearance of an old or antique finish. This can be achieved by various means, such as crackle medium, peeling paint, waxed finish, pigmented varnish, textured paint, or distressed surface.

Anthemion Greek for "flower", this is a classical motif based on a honeysuckle or palm leaf motif radiating from a single point.

Arte povera See Découpage.

Bell flower A classic motif very popular in the eighteenth century, based on bell-shaped flowers hanging in a continuous chain, pendant or swag, and either the same size or graduated. It is similar to the husk motif.

Bleached wood Originally this was the result of decades, or even centuries, of scrubbing wood clean with green soap and sometimes with wet silver sand, or with soft soap and lye. Today this effect can be achieved using wood bleach or it can be simulated by applying white emulsion (possibly thickened with plaster of Paris for a more powdery look) and then lightly washing it off; or by applying a white wax. Both of these techniques work best on woods that have a strong grain.

Bronze powders Very fine metallic powders in a number of gold, copper and silver colours used on furniture over gold size.

Cassone An Italian chest with painted panels, from the Renaissance.

Chinoiserie Chinese-style designs of figures, flowers and small scenes, popular in Europe and America from about the eighteenth century onwards.

Classical A style of motif coming from the classical ancient world of Greece or Rome. The style was revived in the Renaissance and again, as neoclassicism, in the eighteenth century.

Colourwashing A glazing technique using a slow-drying coloured, semi-transparent medium over a coloured base. The glaze is applied and then partly wiped off to give a soft, blurred and cloudy textured effect.

Cornucopia A classical motif based on the horn of plenty. Natural or stylized flowers and fruit topple out of the horn, arranged either naturally or symmetrically.

Crackle glaze/medium Also called the peeling-paint technique, this gives the look of old, cracked paint. It is achieved using a water-based crackle medium between two coats of water-based paint. Each layer is allowed to dry before the next layer is applied.

Crackle varnish To achieve the effect of an Old Master painting on which the varnish has cracked over the years, a water-based varnish is applied over an oil-based varnish when the oil-based one has dried to the point of being a little sticky. A dark-coloured oil paint can be rubbed into the cracks to make them show up.

Découpage Taken from the French term meaning "cut paper", the technique was used from the eighteenth century onwards to decorate furniture. In Italy it is known as *lacca povera* or *arte povera*. Paper cut-outs were also used in country-style work in eastern European countries and in North America.

Distemper A traditional, very matt, chalky, water-based paint made with glue size, ground chalk and pigment.

Distressing Any method of achieving an old, worn look on wood or paintwork, including waxing and crackle effects.

Earth colours Pigments literally taken from the earth, cleaned and pulverized to powder. They include ochres (yellowish pigments), siennas (terracotta pigments), oxides (reddish pigments) and umbers (brownish pigments).

Egg tempera A type of paint made by mixing pigment with egg yolk and a little water. This makes a strong, enduring paint that retains its colour well. It is used in country areas, particularly in Scandinavia and in eastern European countries such as Hungary and Romania.

Faux French word meaning "false" and referring to anything which is painted to look like another material, such as bamboo, wood or marble.

Folk painting Also called country painting, this term is used to describe any style of painting which is either untutored or done according to certain native traditions.

Fresco A wall painting in a water-based medium, often lime water, on wet plaster so the colour penetrates the medium rather than lying on top of it. The technique was used mainly in warm, dry countries such as Italy.

Gesso The base for traditional gilded work and some fine painted furniture, it is made of fine chalk or gypsum mixed with rabbit-skin glue. It is very smooth, fine and absorbent.

Glaze/Glazing A transparent, slow-drying medium, called glaze or scumble, which is coloured and then worked in certain ways to produce one of a large number of techniques, such as wood-graining, marbling, colourwashing or stippling.

Glue There are many uses for glue in decorative painting. Starch-paste glue is used for making print rooms and découpage. Rabbit-skin glue is used for gesso and other animal-based glues. Other glues made from animal bones are called size and are used to make glue paint and distemper. See also Gold size.

Gold size An acrylic- or oil-based glue for sticking metal leaf or bronze powder to a surface; sometimes simply called size.

Graining See Wood-graining.

Grisaille A method of monochromatic painting, usually in shades of grey or pale brown, which was used to make *trompe l'oeil* carved-stone relief panels and medallions from the Renaissance onwards.

Hand-painting Any decoration painted freehand without stencils or other devices.

GLOSSARY

Husk motif See Bell flower.

Incised Decoration made by drawing into wet paint with the end of a brush, to reveal the base coat.

Japan paint/Japanning A paint made initially to copy the colours and glossy finish of imported eastern lacquerwork in the eighteenth century. At first it was a coloured shellac but in the nineteenth century an oil-based version was made.

Lacca povera See Découpage.

Lacquer A varnish made from shellac that dries fast and gives a high shine. See also Sandarac.

Lacquerwork Work often in the Chinese/chinoiserie style, varnished with a high shine using an alcohol/methylated spirit-based varnish such as shellac.

Lattice-work Painted in imitation of open wooden criss-cross or fretwork designs which came from the East; also seen on painted china ware.

Lining Making lines in various patterns and widths on furniture and walls with long-haired brushes.

Lozenge A diamond-shaped motif.

Marbling Using paint to imitate the look of marble; sometimes called faux marble. It can be found in classical and formal settings and also on folk pieces.

Medallion A circular or oval-shaped frame with a motif, often a face or figure, inside.

Metal leaf Aluminium leaf, brass leaf (or Dutch leaf/Dutch metal), gold leaf or silver leaf, which comes in tissue-thin sheets about 10 x 12.5cm (4 x 5in) or 10 x 7.5cm (4 x 3in), in books of 25; applied with gold size. Brass leaf and silver leaf tarnish and so have to be varnished; gold and aluminium leaf do not.

Milk paint A limewash paint made with milk curds to make it strong. Used on furniture and walls.

Oil paint Pigment in an oil medium, used from about the fifteenth century onwards.

Oil varnish A varnish in which the base is oil and the dilutant is white spirit, giving a slightly yellow tint to work.

Parcel gilt Eighteenth-century practice of gilding parts of a frame, carving or item of furniture, sometimes using stencils.

Patera(e) An oval or round shape decorated with a leaf or rosette shape.

Patina The mellow look and feel of an old surface, caused by the build-up of wax and dirt and the discoloration, cracking and flaking of paint and varnish over many years.

Patinating medium A dark, translucent medium for ageing and dulling down any background or painted work. May be a stain, paint wash, wax, or varnish coloured with raw umber or similar pigment.

Pen-and-ink A technique using black ink and a nib pen over sealed wood or white lacquered wood.

Pennsylvania German/Dutch A country style of furniture made by settlers from Germany in the eastern United States during the eighteenth and nineteenth centuries.

Pigments A powdered substance coming from either natural materials (earth, burnt wood, chalk, minerals) or synthetic sources.

Print room Popular in the eighteenth century, a print room was decorated with engravings pasted straight on to the walls, along with paper borders and decorative detailing such as chains, tasselled ropes, ribbons, swags, lions' faces and other classical ornaments.

Rosette A classical motif based on a very stylized flower and used to punctuate painted decoration.

Roundel A round, flat shape with or without additional decoration.

Sandarac A natural resin soluble in alcohol/methylated spirit, used traditionally on Italian and French furniture as a lacquer.

Scrollwork Any design that curves and spirals in a convoluting line.

Shell A classic motif based on a scallop shell; particularly popular in the eighteenth century.

Shellac A natural resin which is soluble in alcohol/methylated spirit and is used for a wide variety of tasks, including French polishing, sealing wood and creating a shiny surface over paintwork.

Size See Glue and Gold size.

Spirit varnish A varnish, usually sandarac or shellac, in which the thinner is alcohol/methylated spirit.

Stamping A way of applying a design on to a surface by printing. This is a modern technique but has precedents in printed fabrics, especially those from India.

Steel wool A mass of very fine wire, also known as wire wool. It is available in various gauges, from very fine for applying wax to very coarse for removing stubborn paint; the medium quality wire can be used for ageing and distressing newly painted furniture.

Stencilling A method of achieving a repeated pattern by wiping or brushing paint over a sheet of card or acetate from which a design has been cut out. The technique has been used on all styles of work, from formal to country pieces.

Stippling A technique using a large stiff-bristled brush in a dabbing action to pounce a glazed and coloured surface while it is still wet, producing a fine, dotty texture.

Strapwork A flat, interlaced design based on plaited, knotted patterns with holes punched in certain parts.

Tempera See Egg tempera.

Trompe l'oeil From the French, meaning "deceive the eye", this is a method of painting using perspective and shadows to achieve a highly realistic, three-dimensional look.

Varnish A protective coat over paintwork. In the past an oil or spirit varnish (see definitions above) was used, but today water-based varnishes are generally substituted.

Water-based varnish A varnish made from acrylic or vinyl; dries very quickly and completely clear.

Wax Beeswax or strong furniture waxes which may include mixtures of paraffin wax as well as carnauba wax obtained from plants.

Wood-graining A paint technique using a coloured glaze over a painted base to imitate the appearance of either a particular wood or a stylized wood.

Places to visit

All Saint's Parish Church
(Ceilings by William Morris)
Church Lane
Middleton Cheney
Nr Banbury
Northamptonshire
OX17 2PB
Tel: (01295) 710 254

American Museum in Britain
Claverton Manor
Bath
BA2 7BD
Tel: (01225) 460 503

Attingham Park
The National Trust
Shrewsbury
Shropshire
SY4 4TP
Tel: (01743) 709 203

Belton House
The National Trust
Grantham
Lincolnshire
NG32 2LS
Tel: (01476) 573 086

Beningbrough Hall
The National Trust
Beningbrough
York
YO30 1DD
Tel: (01904) 470 666

Carl Larsson's House
Carl Larsson Garden
790 15 Sundborn
Sweden
Tel: (023) 60 053

Castle Howard
York
Y060 7DA
Tel: (01653) 648 333

Castletown House
Celbridge
Co. Kildare
Ireland
Tel: (01) 628 8252

Cecil Higgins Art Gallery
Castle Close
Bedford
MK40 3NY
Tel: (01234) 211 222

Charles Rennie Mackintosh
Glasgow School of Art
167 Renfrew Street
Glasgow
Scotland
G3 6RQ
Tel: (0141) 332 9797

Charleston Farmhouse
Near Firle
Lewes
East Sussex
BN8 6LL
Tel: (01323) 811 265

Claridges Hotel
Brook St
Mayfair
London W1A 2JQ
Tel: (0171) 629 8860

Crathes Castle
The National Trust of Scotland
Banchory
Aberdeenshire
Scotland
AB31 5QJ
Tel: (01330) 844 525

Culross Palace
The National Trust of Scotland
West Green House
Fife
Scotland KY12 8JH
Tel: (01383) 880 359

Dalarnas Museum
Stigaregatan 2-5
791 21 Falun
Sweden
Tel: (023) 181 60

Drottningholms Teatermuseum
Filmhuset
Borgvej 5
102 51 Stockholm
Sweden
Tel: (08) 759 0406

Erddig House
The National Trust
Wrexham
Clwydd
Wales
LL13 0YT
Tel: (01978) 355 314

Fenton House
The National Trust
Windmill Hill
Hampstead
NW3 6RT
Tel: (0171) 435 3471

Gladstoneland
The National Trust of Scotland
477 B Lawnmarket
Edinburgh
Scotland
E81 2NT
Tel: (0131) 226 5856

Henry Ford Museum and Greenwich Village
Research Centre
20900 Oakwood Boulevard
Dearborn
Michigan 48121-1970
USA
Tel: (313) 271 1620

Hill House
The National Trust of Scotland
Upper Colquhoun St
Helensburgh
Scotland
G84 9AJ
Tel: (01436) 673 900

Hunterian Art Gallery
The Mackintosh House
University of Glasgow
82 Hillhead Street
Glasgow
Scotland
G12 8QQ
Tel: (0141) 330 5431

Knole House
The National Trust
Knole
Sevenoaks
Kent TN15 0RP
Tel: (01732) 462 100

Neprajzi Museum
Ethnographic Museum Hungary
12th Kossuth Square
Budapest H-1055
Hungary
Tel: (133) 26 340

Nederlands Openluchtmuseum
(Netherlands Open-Air Museum)
Schlemseweg 89
Netherlands
Tel: (085) 57 611

New York State Historical Association
Lake Road
P.O. Box 800
Cooperstown
New York 13326
USA
Tel: (607) 547 1400

Old Sturbridge Village
1 Old Sturbridge Village Road
Sturbridge
Mass. 01 566
USA
Tel: (508) 347 5375

Osterley Park House
The National Trust
Isleworth
Middlesex
TW7 4RB
Tel: (0181) 568 3164

Palazzo Davanzatti
Via Porta Rosa
Florence
Italy
Tel: (55) 21 39 97

Powys Castle
The National Trust
Welshpool
Powys
Wales SY21 8RF
Tel: (01938) 554 336

Royal Pavilion
Brighton
BN1 1EE
Tel: (01273) 290 900

Samode Palace
Dist. Jaipur
Rajasthan
India
Tel: (1423) 4114/4123

Schloss Charlottenhof
Potsdam
Germany
Tel: (331) 969 4228

Schoharie County Historical Society
Old Stone Fort Museum
Complex
Schoharie
New York 12157
USA
Tel: (518) 295 7192

Shelburne Museum
US Route 7
P.O. Box 10
Shelburne
Vermont 05482
USA
Tel: (802) 985 3346

Victoria and Albert Museum
(The room of Chateau
de la Tournerie)
South Kensington
London
SW7 2RL
Tel: (0171) 938 8500

Wightwick Manor
The National Trust
Wightwick Bank
Wolverhampton
WV6 8EE
Tel: (01902) 761 108

Winterthur Museum Garden and Library
Winterthur
Delaware 19735
USA
Tel: (302) 888 4600

Index

Acknowledgements

AUTHOR'S ACKNOWLEDGEMENTS.

I am very grateful to the many people who have helped me research this book. A special thanks goes to all the photographers who helped by giving me information and the curators and staff at museums and houses open to the public. I would also like to thank Nadine Bazar for helping with the picture research and putting me in touch with some of the superb photographers and places. The task of designing the book by sorting, arranging and generally managing all the material was done superbly and endlessly patiently by Christine Wood. The editing was done with magnificent speed and efficiency by Alison Wormleighton. Thanks also goes to all at Collins & Brown, especially Kate Haxell, Cindy Richards and of course, young Tim.

At home, David and the boys, Henry, Felix and Hugo, who have been, as always, endlessly supportive.